Intentional

Intentional

Developing a Deeper Relationship With God

Christina Mayes

Heavenly Places Publishing

Copyright © 2018 by Christina Mayes
All rights reserved
Printed in the United States of America

978-1-7335588-0-8

Published by Heavenly Places Publishing
Boaz, Alabama

Unless otherwise stated, Scripture is taken from the New King James Bible (NKJV),
© 1979, 1980, 1982, Thomas Nelson, Inc., Publishers.

Also used: The Holy Bible, New International Version (NIV), copyright © 1973, 1978, 1984 by International Bible Society.

Also used: The New Living Translation (NLT), copyright © 1996, 2004 by Tyndale House Publishers, Inc., Wheaton, Illinois 60189. All rights reserved.

Also used: King James Version (KJV).

Dedication

All glory and honor goes to God for this book. I just held the pen.

Honor the Lord with your possessions, And with the firstfruits of all your increase; So your barns will be filled with plenty, And your vats will overflow with new wine. Proverbs 3:9-10

Contents

Introduction xi

Devotions

True Worship 1

Why Study? 3

Communication God's Way 5

Serving With God 7

Worship Hymn 9

Learning God's Way 11

What's Your Witness? 13

Constant Communication 15

Worthy of Worship 17

Knowledge and Understanding 18

Being Still 20

Service Minded 24

Worthy of Praise 26

Getting Wisdom 28

Walking the Walk 31

Whatever You Dwell on, You Serve 33

Worship in the Spirit 35

Study to Answer 37

Serving Sacrificially 39

Worship with Reverence 41

Study to Comfort 43

Set Your Heart on Jesus 45

Praying With Thanksgiving 47

The Name Above All Names 49

Studying God's Character 52

Praying With Confidence 55

Serving the Church 57

What Interferes With Worship 59

Studying God's Nature 61

Witness in Waiting 63

Praying in the Spirit 67

What Worship Is Not 70

Learning the Promises of God 72

Praying Scripture 74

Serving the Lost 76

Delight Yourself in the Lord 78

Prerequisites to the Promises 81

Witness in Working 84

Hanging Out With Jesus 87

Christina Mayes

Introduction

INTENTIONAL - done on purpose, deliberate

Authentic means real. Not a copy, not a fake or a knock-off. Real. Being authentic means being intentional. Authentic *doesn't* mean perfect. Let me repeat that. Authentic doesn't mean perfect. We CANNOT be perfect and trying to attain perfection will leave you frazzled and legalistic. It is an unattainable goal for us.

We can, however, be perfect (mature) in Christ. Because we take on the righteousness of Christ when we accept Him as our Savior, we can have perfection before God. It doesn't mean that *we* are perfect. It means that God will accept Christ's perfection for our imperfection. Our responsibility is to pursue the character and nature of Christ so that we learn to be like Him.

We have been bought, redeemed, and saved by Christ's blood. We have chosen to accept His authority over our lives. We are no longer alive because we have been crucified with Christ. Christ is now Lord and commander of our life (Gal 2:20).

Being intentional means that we live in the real world, with real struggles, and real needs that we choose to meet with God's solutions. Being intentional is what having a relationship with Christ is all about. Learning God's ways, His character, and His nature enables us to love God with all our heart, soul, and mind, and love others, just like Him. Why is this important? Because loving Him and loving like Him are our two greatest commandments (Matt 22:36-40).

Intentionally loving God will all our heart, soul, and mind can only be done with help from the Holy Spirit. The Holy Spirit helps us to stay focused on Christ in the middle of our crisis. Intentionally loving others the way that Christ loves us requires that our relationship with Christ be preeminent. We can't love *like* Him if we haven't been *with* Him.

I know the struggle. I've made all the excuses too:

- I'm too tired
- I don't have time
- I don't feel good
- I will later
- We had an emergency
- I can't concentrate/focus
- I overslept/ran late
- I don't know what to do/study

The bottom line is, you have to be intentional in your relationship with Christ. You have to choose Him first. Before your dreams and desires. Before your wants and needs. Before your family, friends, church, job, goals, plans, hobbies, and agenda. Before your day (or night) starts, you have to choose Jesus. It is a choice *you* have to make. Living an intentional life is not easy. It means that when you make that unknown number of decisions every day you will apply God's Word to *your* world, *your* struggles, and *your* needs every second. It will seem time consuming and too much trouble at first, but, if you persevere, God has promised to bless your faithfulness (Gal 6:9, James 1:12).

Intentional living requires sacrifice. I'm not going to sugar-coat anything. You may have to spend less time watching TV or scrolling on your phone. You will have to stop, drop, and pray before you respond. You will have to ask forgiveness, and give it, when you don't *feel* like it. You will have to crucify that selfish sin nature within every time it rears its ugly head. You will be exhausted from battling yourself and modeling Christ to others. But then, you will renew your strength in the Lord, and it will all have been worth it.

True Worship

Therefore, I urge you, brothers and sisters, in view of God's mercy, to offer your bodies as a living sacrifice, holy and pleasing to God—this is your true and proper worship. Romans 12:1

In the Old Testament, worship of God included animal sacrifices for the atonement of sins. Because Jesus became the final and ultimate sacrifice for all sins, animals are no longer required or sufficient.

The Bible tells us in Romans 12:1 to: "offer our bodies [everything that we are] as a living sacrifice" as part of our worship of God in response to God's mercies [the benefits we receive as children of God].

True Worship requires a sacrifice. Your sacrifice may be time, money, resources, attitude, control, pride -- the list could go on forever. Our sacrifice, whatever it is, is meant to enable us to focus more completely on Jesus so that the Holy Spirit can revive and renew us. Making us more like Jesus, and developing within us the fruits of the Spirit, True Worship helps us to think and to act God's way each day.

Prayer: Jesus, you alone are worthy of worship and praise. Thank you for working in me through the Holy Spirit to make me more like you. Show me what you'd have me sacrifice in order to worship you in Spirit and in truth. Enable me to act God's way so that you are glorified. In Jesus' name, amen.

Ask: How can I be a living sacrifice?

_____

_____

_____

Apply: Today I will sacrifice

_____

_____

_____

Reflect: What happened? Tell your story. How did your sacrifice change your life?

_____

_____

_____

_____

_____

Why Study?

All Scripture is God-breathed and is useful for teaching, rebuking, correcting and training in righteousness, so that the servant of God may be thoroughly equipped for every good work. 2 Timothy 3:16-17

Why do we have to study this? Across the country (and around the world) countless students from elementary through college are asking this question. The answer -- to learn. Studying is practicing new concepts and skills so that they become part of your abilities. The more you practice them, the easier they are to use.

When we apply this same concept to the Bible, we can see tremendous application opportunities and real change evidenced in our lives. We begin with communicating with Jesus about where He wants to work in our life. We search the Word of God for examples of what to do (or what NOT to do) and then begin to apply the principles God brings out to our situation. Then we practice, practice, practice.

Prayer: Jesus, thank you for the change you are making in my life and the life of others through me. Show me where You want to start working. Enable me to practice the skills and concepts You want to teach me so that I may glorify You. In Jesus' name, amen.

Ask: What principles does God want me to learn?

_____

_____

_____

Apply: Jesus, teach me to

_____

_____

_____

Reflect: What happened? Tell the story of what Jesus is teaching you.

_____

_____

_____

_____

_____

Communication God's Way

But the Helper, the Holy Spirit, whom the Father will send in my name, he will teach you all things and bring to your remembrance all that I have said to you. John 14:26

God communicates in specific ways. We don't necessarily get a phone call or an email from Him, but He can use a phone call from a friend or an email with a devotional to communicate with us. Three ways that God can communicate with us are through His Word, through prayer, and through the Holy Spirit. If we want to communicate with God, we have to use His methods.

Spending time in God's Word is an easy and dependable way to communicate with God. Going to the Word and reading it in context helps us to understand who God is and what He wants to tell us. Prayer is another way to communicate with God. When we pray, we can have a conversation with God. I like to write my conversations down, especially if I am upset about something. His answers are evident when I go back and reread our conversation.

Finally, God's go-to man is the Holy Spirit. The Holy Spirit can: communicate for us when we don't know what to say (Romans 8:26), use a fellow Christian to keep us accountable (Galatians 6:1-2), and reach us through a song when nothing else seems to work (Colossians 3:16). Be open to communication God's way so that you don't miss an important message!

Prayer: Jesus, open my spiritual eyes and ears to receive your messages. Keep my heart tender toward you do that I do not hinder the work of your Holy Spirit. In Jesus' name, amen.

Ask: What is God trying to communicate to me right now?

_____

_____

_____

Apply: Jesus, I am listening. What do you want to tell me?

_____

_____

_____

Reflect: What happened? Tell the story of what Jesus told you.

_____

_____

_____

_____

_____

Serving With God

Obey the Lord and serve him faithfully with all your heart. Remember the great things he has done for you. 1 Samuel 12:24

The Bible promises that the one who serves God will be honored. Now, we know that receiving honor is not our motivation for serving God, right? I guess it just depends on if we are serving FOR God or WITH God. Many serving FOR God *do* seek to be honored by men. (Matthew 6:5) While most serving WITH God are fine with remaining behind-the-scenes because they experience God's honor in their hearts.

This doesn't apply to all who are serving, but it does prompt us to evaluate our own service. What is my motivation? Why am I serving in this position? Am I serving WITH God or FOR God?

Prayer: Jesus, thank you for helping me understand what serving you means. Examine my motivations, Lord, and remove any selfish influences. Lead me to the service opportunities YOU have for me. In Jesus' name, amen.

Ask: Where is Jesus leading me to serve with Him?

_____

_____

_____

Apply: Jesus wants me to

_____

_____

_____

Reflect: What happened? Tell your story of your obedience to the Holy Spirit's prompting?

_____

_____

_____

_____

_____

_____

Worship Hymn

Oh come, let us sing to the Lord; let us make a joyful noise to the rock of our salvation! Let us come into his presence with thanksgiving; let us make a joyful noise to him with songs of praise! Psalm 95:1-2

Most of us have a particular song or hymn that we love. Something that speaks to our heart, our situation, or our redemption. I know that I have a standing list of songs when I need comfort or encouragement, when I want to shout praises, and when I desire to reverently worship God.

Worship hymns are not new. Songs of worship have been recorded since the book of Genesis. The Bible tells us to sing songs of praise and worship to God. (Psalms 104:33-34) This is especially important during trials. Satan hates nothing more than when we continue to sing praises to God even in the midst of our trials. But remember, others are listening. (Acts 16:25) Your worship of God, particularly in trying times, speaks with louder volume than when things are going well.

Prayer: Jesus, thank you for the gift of music to strengthen and encourage us. Remind me to count the cost when I sing praises to your name. In Jesus' name, amen.

Ask: How can I praise God today?

_____

_____

_____

Apply: Make a playlist, on paper or on a device, of the songs God uses to comfort, encourage, and revive you, then sing them to the Lord with a thankful heart.

_____

_____

_____

Reflect: What happened? Tell your story behind one of your worship hymns?

_____

_____

_____

_____

_____

_____

Learning God's Way

*I will instruct you and teach you in the way you should go;
I will counsel you with my loving eye on you. Psalm 32:8*

As a teacher, I know that learning styles differ. One student may need to work with his hands, another may need lots of visuals, and another may need to listen closely to a lecture or video. Trying to integrate all the different learning styles and ability levels is a challenge all teachers face. Christ, however, had no trouble teaching people and meeting their needs. He met them where they were, got on their level, and changed their lives.

When we choose to learn God's way, we can trust that He will do all the heavy lifting. There is no need to worry that we won't understand or that He will be a harsh taskmaster. The Bible promises us in Matthew 11:28-30:

> **28** "Come to me, all you who are weary and burdened, and I will give you rest. **29** Take my yoke upon you and learn from me, for I am gentle and humble in heart, and you will find rest for your souls. **30** For my yoke is easy and my burden is light."

Prayer: Heavenly Father, thank you for Your Word and for taking the time to teach me. Open my mind and my heart to all that you want me to learn. In Jesus' name, amen.

Ask: Jesus, how can I understand you better?

_____

_____

_____

Apply: Read Luke 15:1-32. What is the main idea?

_____

_____

_____

Reflect: What happened? Tell your story of what the Holy Spirit revealed to you in God's Word.

_____

_____

_____

_____

_____

_____

What's Your Witness?

Only let your manner of life be worthy of the gospel of Christ, so that whether I come and see you or am absent, I may hear of you that you are standing firm in one spirit, with one mind striving side by side for the faith of the gospel, Philippians 1:27

What do people say about you? Do you have the reputation of being a good ambassador of the kingdom? What witness are you demonstrating to others by your actions and words? The Bible tells us to be known by our love in John 13:35. Not only are we to be known by our love but also by our testimony (Acts 26:16). The Bible says that God keeps a record of all we say and do and that we will give an account of every idle word spoken and every work (Matthew 12:36, 1 Corinthians 3:13).

Your witness is important because others are watching. They want to see what kind of God it is you serve. This can be very sobering! Not only are God and others watching, they are keeping a record! Therefore, live according to Matthew 5:16, as follows:

"In the same way, let your light shine before others, that they may see your good deeds and glorify your Father in heaven."

Prayer: Jesus, thank you for saving me. Guide me to use my testimony as a witness to Your endless love, matchless grace, and infinite mercy. Forgive me for all the times I have brought shame and darkness on Your Name through my thoughtless words and actions. Enable me to bring honor to Your Name and light to those in need of You so that You may be glorified. In Jesus' name, amen.

Ask: Jesus, what words and actions do I need to change so that I can honor You?

_____

_____

_____

Apply: Jesus, with your help, I will

_____

_____

_____

Reflect: What happened? Tell the story of how you changed and what the result was.

_____

_____

_____

_____

_____

Constant Communication

My sheep listen to my voice; I know them, and they follow me. John 10:27

Many people today have a cellular phone. This device allows them to be in constant communication with their friends, family, work, and the world. We have access to any and all types of information and can communicate via phone, text, tweet, or post. In fact, there is such a huge attachment to these devices that commercials are now being created to support "device-free" meals and activities.

We thought that having the ability to contact someone at any time, anywhere, especially in an emergency, was a good idea. Then we thought that being able to access information in the same way was also good. However, it seems to have become more of a distraction in most cases. The Bible says in 1 Thessalonians 5:17 to "pray without ceasing". If I am going to be in constant communication with someone, it should be my Heavenly Father. I have to ask myself a few questions: Did I talk to Him as long as I talked to others? Did I spend as much time sending Him messages as I did my friends and family? Did I read as many of His posts as I did of others on my social media app? Consider your ways and repent if necessary. I'll see you at the altar.

Prayer: Jesus, thank you that I can be in constant communication with You. Forgive me for letting other distractions replace my time with you. Empower me to honor and respect you by investing in time with you. In Jesus' name, amen.

Ask: What distractions do I need to put aside so that I can focus on you?

___

Apply: Jesus, I commit to spending time with you. I will

___

Reflect: What happened? Tell the story of what happened when you met with God.

___

Worthy of Worship

Come, let's worship him and bow down. Let's kneel before the Lord who made us, Psalm 95:6

One of the songs we sing at church is Worthy of Worship. The words of the hymn fill me with reverence and awe for my Savior and Redeemer. I love the lilting melody and sing it with all my heart. Its words always remind me why Jesus is so worthy of worship and praise. He is our Father, Creator, Master and Lord. Jesus is the King of all kings and my Redeemer. He is a Wonderful Counselor, Comforter, and Friend. Jesus is my Savior and the source of my eternal life. How can I not worship Him? He alone is worthy. No one else took my place on the cross or paid my penalty for sin, a debt I could not pay. I didn't just get a Savior, I got a Sustainer. Someone who would strengthen and support me physically, mentally, emotionally, financially and spiritually. Jesus was worthy of worship inherently, but my worship of Him is because of what He did, and continues to do, for me.

Prayer: Holy Father, I thank you and praise you. You alone are worthy of worship and honor. Please forgive me of my sins and guide me to worship you with all of my heart, all of my focus, and all that I have. In Jesus' name, amen.

Ask: Am I honoring God with my worship?

_____

_____

_____

_____

Apply: Jesus, how do you want me to honor you in worship?

_____

_____

_____

Reflect: What happened? Tell the story of how you honored God with your worship.

_____

_____

_____

_____

_____

_____

Knowledge and Understanding

For the LORD gives wisdom; from his mouth come knowledge and understanding. Proverbs 2:6

The words knowledge and understanding are often interchangeable. Their definitions are so similar that they are used to describe each other! The words are almost identical twins, but, if we really break them down to their core, they have deeper differences than we often give them credit for. Knowledge is facts, information, and skills. These can all be obtained without any understanding. Students can memorize facts, information, and skills and have no real understanding of them because understanding is the ability to demonstrate the use of (or the application of) knowledge. Having knowledge is great, but how are you using it? Do you understand its purpose and why it's important? Take the apostrophe for example. You know what it is but do you know how to apply it? Do you understand it? Its purpose is to indicate possession or the presence of a contraction. However, it is greatly misused to show plurality.

The Bible also lists knowledge and understanding separately knowing that each is important. For instance, in Proverbs 1:7 it says, "The fear of the Lord is the beginning of knowledge, but fools despise wisdom and instruction." Then in Proverbs 9:10 it says, "The fear of the Lord is the beginning of wisdom, and the knowledge of the Holy One is understanding." Wisdom's words are "plain to him who understands, and right to those who find knowledge." (Proverbs 8:9)

Prayer: Holy Father, thank you for opening my eyes and ears to the knowledge contained in Your Word. Help me to understand it so that I use it wisely to help grow your kingdom. In Jesus' name, amen.

Ask: Am I using knowledge and understanding wisely?

_____

_____

_____

Apply: Jesus, how would you have me handle the knowledge and understanding you have given me of Your Word?

_____

_____

_____

Reflect: What happened? Tell the story of how you used knowledge in an understanding way.

_____

_____

_____

_____

_____

_____

Being Still

Delight yourself also in the Lord, and He shall give you the desires of your heart. Psalm 37:4

Being still is hard. Like real hard. Because even if we manage to make our body still, our mind is not as cooperative. And, if you have ADD or ADHD, well, only others who suffer along with you can possibly understand! Yet, the Bible tells us three different times to be still.

He says, "Be still, and know that I am God;

> I will be exalted among the nations,
> I will be exalted in the earth." (Psalm 46:10)

The Lord will fight for you; you need only to be still." (Exodus 14:14)

> Be still before the Lord
>   and wait patiently for him;
> do not fret when people succeed in their ways,
> when they carry out their wicked schemes. (Psalm 37:7)

In Psalm 46:10, God's instruction is meant as "stop fighting". Anyone with children or working with children knows that they fight constantly, and not even with each other. Sometimes it's just with themselves! I know you're nodding your head in agreement but, you do that too. Just ask God if he hasn't already convicted you.

The next instance is Exodus 14:14. Here the Lord reminds us that the battle is His and that He will fight for us. He only wants us to be still. Sometimes, there is nothing we can do to save ourselves from whatever situation we are in, or, if we try to do something, it will make the situation worse. In this instance, we must demonstrate our trust by allowing God to fight for us. If you are as attached to being in control as I am, it can be *really* hard to let go of the situation. Often, however, that is the only way it can be resolved.

Finally, Psalm 37:7 tells us to be still and wait patiently for the Lord to act on our behalf. He says "Don't worry about, or be envious of, those evil people prospering from wicked schemes." Focus. On. The. Lord. Like I said, being still is hard work! We look around and see other people getting what *we* want and so we start to question. When me God? Why not now? Instead of questioning and complaining, like we usually do, we need to start praising and thanking Him for what we already have and what He's already done. Being still becomes easy when we are focused on being thankful and grateful, trusting Him to bring to pass what is best for us.

Pray: Holy Father, thank you for protecting me from what I can't see and don't know. Jesus, I praise you and know that your timing is perfect. Thank you for guarding me from harm. Lord, I may not like it or understand it, but I can trust you have a good plan for me. A plan to prosper me and not harm me, that provides me with hope and a future. I trust You to know what's best for me. In Jesus' name, amen.

Ask: Jesus, what do I need to let You handle while I remain still and patient before You?

_____
_____
_____

Apply: Jesus, I give you

_____
_____
_____

Handle it as only You can.

Reflect: What happened? Tell the story of how God is working in your situation.

_____
_____
_____
_____
_____

Service Minded

Do not be shaped by this world; instead be changed within by a new way of thinking. Then you will be able to decide what God wants for you; you will know what is good and pleasing to him and what is perfect.
Romans 12:2

There are a lot of things going around about changing your mindset. Instead of negative self-talk, you are supposed to "change your mindset" to the positive. For example if you can't do that math problem, you are supposed to change your mind to say "I can't do this math problem YET." I will agree that changing your mindset can help you have a more positive outlook, and then that positivity will help you to persevere until you can complete the task.

Along with a positive mindset we also need a service mindset. Not necessarily a mindset that we are always required to say "yes" to every service opportunity, but the mindset that is tapped-in to the Father so that we don't miss an opportunity to serve with Him.

Prayer: Heavenly Father, thank you for the privilege of serving alongside You. Change my mindset to one of service so that I don't miss any opportunities to sow seeds of Your love. Direct me to the specific service You have for me today. In Jesus' name, amen.

Intentional

Ask: What will you do today in service with God?

_____

_____

_____

Apply: Today I will

_____

_____

_____

Reflect: What happened? Tell the story of your service opportunity with God.

_____

_____

_____

_____

_____

_____

_____

Worthy of Praise

Great is the LORD, and highly to be praised, And His greatness is unsearchable. Psalm 145:3

We all like to be praised. Praise indicates that we are "approved of" or admired. For some people, it is being told "thank you" for all the hard work they have done. I like when I am praised for good work but I love when I am rewarded for it. My reward doesn't have to be monetary or public praise, although those are nice. My favorite reward is security. Does that sound weird? To some I'm sure it does, but to me it sounds wonderful. Safe in my position, safe in my ability, and safe in my superiority. As someone who has always felt inferior, I work hard to be the best at whatever I do so that I can be rewarded with praises, which for me equals security. Jesus, however, is worthy of praise. By birth I am not worthy. I have to do something to earn praise. But, Jesus is worthy. He already has qualities that merit recognition and, as if that wasn't enough, He took it a step further and added *actions* that were worthy of praise. We can and should praise Jesus for who He already is but we should also praise Him for what He has done. He is worthy.

Prayer: Jesus, we praise you and thank you for who you are and what you have done. No other person is worthy of honor and glory. Remind us Lord to praise you always. In Jesus' name, amen.

Intentional

Ask: Have I taken time to truly praise Jesus today?

Apply: Take a moment to write out your praise of Jesus right now. Jesus I want to praise you for:

Reflect: What happened? Tell the story of how praising Him changed you.

Getting Wisdom

Get wisdom and understanding. Don't forget or ignore my words.
Proverbs 4:5

In the book of Proverbs, the first four chapters are dedicated to wisdom. Getting it, having it, finding it, keeping it, and using it are all topics discussed. Also, Proverbs tells us what will happen if we find wisdom and use it appropriately. We can expect blessings, prosperity, honor, life, grace, safety, comfort, and confidence. Why? Wisdom enables us to make good choices and decisions that will cause us to prosper.

So, how do you get wisdom? You cannot buy it at the market or borrow it from a library or a friend. Getting wisdom requires the action on your part of stepping out of your comfort zone and experiencing that which you desire wisdom in. For example, if you want to be a wise teacher, find good mentors and work with them. Gain knowledge and understanding by asking questions, but also work closely with them to see how they handle situations and people. Direct experience cannot be replaced by reading books or attending classes.

When we read the Bible we are given the opportunity to learn from the mistakes of others. However, those lessons rarely impact our lives as considerably as the lessons we learn the hard way through direct experience. Still the Bible screams "Get Wisdom! Get Understanding!" (Proverbs 4:5a) "Wisdom is the principal thing; Therefore get wisdom. And in all your getting, get understanding." (Proverbs 4:7) Even though getting wisdom might be painful at times, pain is a powerful motivator for a transformed life. Go get some wisdom.

Prayer: Jesus, I thank You for being the Word so that I can get wisdom and grow in knowledge and understanding. Thank You for the examples You have given us to learn from and live by. Enable me to learn from my mistakes and live a life that honors You. In Jesus' name, amen.

Ask: In what area is God directing me to "get wisdom?"

_____

_____

_____

Apply: Jesus, I know that you want me to get wisdom in

_____

_____

_____

Lead me to the people and places I need so that I can grow in wisdom.

Reflect: What happened? Tell the story of where Christ led you to gain wisdom and how you were transformed.

_____

_____

_____

_____

_____

_____

_____

Walking the Walk

Who is wise and understanding among you? By his good conduct let him show his works in the meekness of wisdom. James 3:13

We have all heard the cliché, "If you are going to talk the talk, you have to walk the walk." This means that our words should line up with our actions. Talking the talk is all well and good but to use another cliché, "Where the rubber meets the road is where it's really at!" People may listen for a while but what they really want is to see. Do you *live* that way? Do you *practice* what you are preaching? Think of it this way, if you are "walking the walk" you probably don't have to "talk the talk" because your actions speak much louder that your words.

Being an effective witness means that what we do and how we respond is more important than what we say. The Bible tells us that our conversation should always be full of grace and seasoned with salt, so that we know how to answer everyone. (Col 4:6) Our speech is important because the power of life and death are in the tongue. (Proverbs 18:21) But many will argue that saying something is easier that doing something.

Prayer: Jesus, enable me to live my life as an effective witness to Your great grace, powerful love, and unending mercy. Help me to demonstrate Your love to my brothers and sisters in Christ and to this lost and hurting world. In Jesus' name, amen.

Ask: Is my witness (my walk) lining up with my testimony (my talk)?

_____
_____
_____

Apply: Spend time in prayer to find out what God wants you to change in order to be a more effective witness.

_____
_____
_____

Reflect: What happened? Tell the story of how God helped you become a more effective witness and what resulted.

_____
_____
_____
_____
_____

Whatever You Dwell on, You Serve

"You must not have any other gods except me." Exodus 20:3

I recently found an index card that I was using as a bookmark in a Bible study book. It said "Whatever you dwell on, you serve." That was a convicting card! I had set my heart on having a particular job, but God said no. "Whatever you dwell on, you serve." God knew that I would make an idol of that job and He will tolerate no idols before Him. Initially my heart sank because I really wanted that job, but as the days went by, the more I thought about it, the more I accepted that He was right. I just didn't want to admit it to myself. Isn't that the case many times? When we are creating or confronted about idols in our lives we deny, deny, deny. "It's not true," or "No I'm not," and "You don't understand" are some of our responses. However, if we will admit it, deep down we know the truth.

Whatever You Dwell On, You Serve.

Prayer: Jesus, forgive me for creating idols before You. Show me my idols, dismantle them, and keep me from creating more. Enable me through Your Word and the Holy Spirit to dwell on You and You only. In Jesus' name, amen.

Ask: What are the idols in my life that you want to clean out?

_____
_____
_____

Apply: Jesus I acknowledge that I have made an idol of:

_____
_____
_____

Reflect: What happened? Tell the story of how Jesus set you free of an idol (s).

_____
_____
_____
_____
_____
_____
_____

Worship in the Spirit

"God is spirit, and those who worship him must worship in spirit and truth." John 4:24

We are made in the image of God. The Trinity of Father, Son, and Holy Spirit is reflected in our body, soul, and mind. In the Bible, (John 4:21-24), Jesus tells the Samaritan woman that the Father is seeking worshipers to worship Him in spirit and in truth. What does that mean?

Worshipping in the spirit means that it is Holy Spirit enabled. {You can't truly worship a God you have not accepted.] When we accept Christ as our Savior and Redeemer, we are given the Holy Spirit as a guide and comforter. The Holy Spirit leads us into true, authentic worship of God. He enables us to come before God with sincerity of heart. Also, since God is spirit, we can worship Him anytime or anywhere, we are not restricted to a building, day of the week, or time of the day. God is always there, ready when we are.

Prayer: Holy Spirit, thank you for preparing me to worship God. Soften my heart so that I can worship You in spirit and in truth in ways that are pleasing to You. In Jesus' name, amen.

Ask: Am I worshiping God or just going through the motions for the benefit of other?

Apply: Answer the question. Repent if necessary. Make a plan that will support you in worshipping God authentically.

Reflect: What happened? Tell the story of how your worship changed in response to what God spoke to your heart.

Study to Answer

"but in your hearts honor Christ the Lord as holy, always being prepared to make a defense to anyone who asks you for a reason for the hope that is in you; yet do it with gentleness and respect," 1 Peter 3:15

If you are like me, there have been times when you didn't study for a test. For whatever reason, you were not prepared to give an answer. When that happens in school it can result in a bad grade and possibly more work to compensate for that failure. The same thing can happen in life, but usually with harsher consequences. Thankfully, we have the Bible to guide us.

The Bible is the "answer key" to the test of life and, thanks to Jesus, it is an open book test! We can study it, absorb it, memorize it, learn from it, and be ready to give an answer when we are tested through various trials. James 1:2-3 states: "My brethren, count it all joy when you fall into various trials, knowing that the testing of your faith produces patience"(endurance).

The more tests and trials you complete, the greater endurance you build. Study so that you know what you believe, why you believe it, and why it is beneficial for others to believe. The **Truth** of God's Word will remain the truth in all circumstances.

Prayer: Jesus, "Your word is a lamp to my feet and a light to my path." Thank you for Your Word. Help me to study and apply Your Word to my heart so that I am prepared to give an answer of the hope I have in you. In Jesus' name, amen.

Ask: Why do I study the Bible? What do I believe and why do I believe that?

_____

_____

_____

Apply: Answer the "Ask" questions and provide at least three scripture references, in context, to support your answers.

_____

_____

_____

Reflect: What happened? Tell the story of what God revealed to you.

_____

_____

_____

_____

_____

_____

Serving Sacrificially

Therefore, I urge you, brothers and sisters, in view of God's mercy, to offer your bodies as a living sacrifice, holy and pleasing to God—this is your true and proper worship. Romans 12:1

When we choose to serve others for God we are sacrificing our time, talents, and resources to Him. He gave to us and we are giving back to Him. Our attitude in serving Him is what makes our actions an obligation or a sweet smelling sacrifice.

Doing good is not always easy. Sometimes we encounter difficult people, dangerous circumstances, or discouragement, but, maintaining a servant-hearted attitude helps us to overcome through Christ.

Whenever you start to feel discouraged or overwhelmed by all that needs to be done, step back, refocus on Jesus, and remember who and why you are serving sacrificially.

Prayer: Holy Father, thank you for enabling me to serve you sacrificially. Keep my heart tender toward you. Jesus, please help me to focus on You whenever I feel overwhelmed or discouraged. Thank you for the Holy Spirit's guard over my attitude. In Jesus' name, amen.

Ask: Is my service a sweet smelling sacrifice or an odorous obligation?

_____

_____

_____

Apply: Speak with God about your current serving situation, does He want you to continue? Is He prompting you to do something else? Be obedient to whatever He tells you.

_____

_____

_____

Reflect: What happened? Tell the story of how you were obedient of God.

_____

_____

_____

_____

_____

_____

Worship with Reverence

"Therefore, since we are receiving a kingdom that cannot be shaken, let us be thankful, and so worship God acceptably with reverence and awe," Hebrews 12:28

Worship is defined as the feeling or expression of reverence and adoration for a duty. Reverence is deep respect for someone or something. What has your worship been like recently? Are you just doing what everybody else is doing or are you meditating on your deep respect and love for Christ? Worship, even corporate, is meant to be personal. How is the song or message connecting *you* to the Savior? Are you focusing on Him and what He is trying to communicate to you?

The Bible mentions how we are to revere God and Christ, (Isaiah 25:3; Ps 22:23; Job 37:24; Lev 19:32; Deut 13:4; Mal 4:2; 1 Peter 3:15; Deut 4:10), it also explains what happens when there is a lack of reverence (Hosea 10:3; Deut 28:58-59; Isaiah 63:17). Be sure that you follow God's commands and worship in sincere reverence. Examine yourself as the Bible says in 1 Corinthians 11:27-29 so that you are worshipping in a worthy and reverent manner.

Prayer: Holy Father, forgive me of my sins and cleanse my heart. Enable me to worship You with the reverence You deserve. In Jesus' name, amen.

Ask: How can I demonstrate my deep reverence for You, Lord?

_____

_____

_____

Apply: In your next worship experience, intentionally focus on God and allow Him to lead your worship of Him.

_____

_____

_____

Reflect: What happened? Tell the story of how your worship experience changed when you let God lead.

_____

_____

_____

_____

_____

_____

_____

Study to Comfort

Praise be to the God and Father of our Lord Jesus Christ, the Father of compassion and the God of all comfort, 4 who comforts us in all our troubles, so that we can comfort those in any trouble with the comfort we ourselves receive from God. 2 Corinthians 1:3-4

There seems to be no other time when we seek the counsel of scripture more than when we need comfort. When we are hurting, anxious, or afraid, God's voice of comfort is what we long to hear. Studying to find comfort not only benefits us, but also others that will cross our path with a similar issue.

Sometimes, God allows trials in our lives because He knows that we will be in a strategic position to encourage someone else with His Word and our personal testimony of His faithfulness in dark and trying times. Study to find comfort and encouragement for yourself. But, also be ready to encourage and comfort others with the same comfort that God has given you so that He may be glorified. (2 Cor 1:4)

Prayer: Holy Father, thank you for Your comfort and encouragement, enable me to be a light and a comfort to someone else so that you are glorified. In Jesus' name, amen.

Ask: How can I comfort someone today?

_____

_____

_____

Apply: Pray and ask God to send you someone to comfort through His Word and your testimony. Be on the look-out for who He sends!

_____

_____

_____

Reflect: What happened? Tell the story of how you helped to comfort another through Christ.

_____

_____

_____

_____

_____

_____

_____

Set Your Heart on Jesus

Since, then, you have been raised with Christ, set your hearts on things above, where Christ is, seated at the right hand of God. Set your minds on things above, not on earthly things. For you died, and your life is now hidden with Christ in God. When Christ, who is your life, appears, then you also will appear with him in glory. Colossians 3:1-4

When I first read these words I was pretty sure I understood their meaning. When I looked up the phrase to verify my contextual understanding, the synonym "want desperately" exploded off the page before me. Could I replace "set your heart on" with "want desperately?" Was there evidence in my life that I desperately wanted Jesus?

If you asked my friends, family, or others that knew me what was one thing I wanted desperately, what would they say? The top answer probably would not be Jesus. Why is that, you ask? Most likely because I have been too focused on what I don't have, and not thankful enough for what I do have.

Would the people who know **you** say that one thing you "want desperately" is Jesus? If not, then let us all refocus and make Jesus our top priority.

Prayer: Jesus, I admit I have not set my heart on You. Please forgive me. Thank You for Your love, mercy, and especially grace. Rekindle my passion for You and restore Yourself as my first love. Make me fervent for You. In Jesus' name, amen.

Ask: What does it look like in real life to "desperately want Jesus"?

_____

_____

_____

Apply: Jesus I know demonstrating my desperation for You is more than a t-shirt, necklace, or bumper sticker. Today I will:

_____

_____

_____

Reflect: What happened? Tell the story of what wanting Jesus desperately looks like in your life.

_____

_____

_____

_____

_____

_____

Praying With Thanksgiving

Do not be anxious about anything, but in every situation, by prayer and petition, with thanksgiving, present your requests to God.
Philippians 4:6

Want a fast track, first-in-line audience with the King? Pray with Thanksgiving. Nothing clears the aisles quicker than having a thankful and grateful heart. Philippians 4:6 says,

> "Do not be anxious about anything, but in every situation, by prayer and petition, with thanksgiving, present your requests to God."

When we pray with a thankful and grateful heart our entire attitude changes because we have shifted our focus from ourselves onto God. Our "self" is worried, anxious, afraid, hurt, angry, desperate, or other. Praying with thanksgiving helps us to move from "self" to Savior. When that happens we can receive Philippians 4: 7,

> "And the peace of God, which transcends all understanding, will guard your hearts and your minds in Christ Jesus."

Prayer: Jesus, I just want to thank you, [Begin your list of "thank-you's" here]. In Jesus' name, amen.

Ask: How can I demonstrate my thankfulness:

_____

_____

_____

Apply: Sing "Jesus, We Just Want To Thank You":

https://video.search.yahoo.com/yhs/search;_ylt=AwrC3TQ6YgFcpWcAF5EPxQt.;_ylu=X3oDM TByMjB0aG5zBGNvbG8DYmYxBHBvcwMxBHZ0aWQDBHNlYwNzYw-- ?p=lyrics+jesus+we+just+want+to+thank+you&fr=yhs-iba-1&hspart=iba&hsimp=yhs-1

> Jesus, we just want to thank You,
> Jesus, we just want to thank You,
> Jesus, we just want to thank You,
> Thank You for being so good.
>
> Jesus, we just want to praise You,
> Jesus, we just want to praise You,
> Jesus, we just want to praise You,
> Praise You for being so good.
>
> Savior, we just want to serve You,
> Savior, we just want to serve You,
> Savior, we just want to serve You,
> Serve You for being so good.

Reflect: What happened? Tell the story of how praying with thanksgiving changed you.

_____

_____

_____

The Name Above All Names

Therefore God also has highly exalted Him and given Him the name which is above every name, that at the name of Jesus every knee should bow, of those in heaven, and of those on earth, and of those under the earth, and that every tongue should confess that Jesus Christ is Lord, to the glory of God the Father. Philippians 2:9-11

Jesus. There is no other name by which we can be saved (Acts 4:12).

He is our Advocate (1 John 2:1)

The Author and Perfecter of our faith (Hebrews 12:2)

Our Bread of Life (John 6:35)

Our Deliverer (1 Thessalonians 1:10)

The Good Shepherd (John 10:11)

Our Great High Priest (Hebrews 4:14)

The Holy Servant of God (Acts 4:29-30)

The I Am (John 8:58)

The King of Kings and Lord of Lords (Revelations 17:14)

The precious Lamb of God (John 1:29)

The Light of the World (John 8:12)

Our Mediator (1 Timothy 2:5)

The Messiah (John 1:41)

The Resurrection and the Life (John 11:25)

The Way to God (John 14:6)

The Lord of All (Phil 2:9-11)

I could go on and on listing references to all that Jesus is, to and for us. Each of these names are important and many are incredibly dear. When you are worshipping, remember and meditate on the Name Above All Names, Jesus.

Prayer: Jesus, You alone are worthy of praise, honor, and glory. Thank You for being my Deliverer and Advocate. Lord I praise You for being my Bread of Life and my Good Shepherd. I worship You as the Lamb of God, the Holy Servant, and My Great High Priest. You are all I need. I am so grateful that You alone are the Author and Perfecter of my faith. In Jesus' name, amen.

Ask: How does understanding the different names of God help me to understand His character?

___

Apply: Create a personal prayer using the Names of Jesus that are speaking to your situation right now.

___

Reflect: What happened? Tell the story or write your prayer here.

Studying God's Character

"For I, the Lord, do not change; therefore you, O sons of Jacob, are not consumed." Malachi 3:6

If you are writing a story with characters, those characters are expected to have an arc, or transformation, over time. In the Bible, we have many examples of characters arcing, sometimes positively and sometimes negatively. One difference is God. He never changes and He never will.

As a writer, you want your character to grow as a person and come out better on the other side of whatever challenge they faced, because it means there is hope that you can too. But with God, He is the standard. He is already all that needs to be. This is why He is to be our measuring stick, not other people. Other people are still arcing.

When we study the character of God, His righteousness, His holiness, His goodness, etc., we can see the picture of what He wants to make us into. We can also see why He is worthy of our trust in Him. He is never going to change. He is never going to fail. He is never going to do anything other than what is best for us. Study the character of God so that you understand who He is and what He wants from you. Then you won't be deceived by imitation gods.

Prayer: Holy Father, I am so thankful and grateful that You never change. Help me study Your character and understand how You want to make me into the likeness of You. Protect me from being deceived by imitators of You Lord. In Jesus' name, amen.

Ask: Do I understand the character of God?

Apply: Choose an attribute of God (or more than one) and do an in-depth study. Answer these questions:
- What is the attribute?
- What does it mean?
- How does God epitomize that attribute?
- How does it apply/how can I apply it to my life?

Reflect: What happened? Tell the story of what you learned.

Praying With Confidence

"Now this is the confidence that we have in Him, that if we ask anything according to His will, He hears us. And if we know that He hears us, whatever we ask, we know that we have the petitions that we have asked of Him." (1 John 5:14-15)

Ever feel uncertain when you are praying? Me too. I think if we are all honest, there are many times that we pray doubting. We don't really mean to, but sometimes the situation seems so hopeless we get overwhelmed by the impossibility and forget that "with God all things are possible" (Matthew 19:26).

John tells us that we can be confident when approaching God with our requests.

> "Now this is the confidence that we have in Him, that if we ask anything according to His will, He hears us. And if we know that He hears us, whatever we ask, we know that we have the petitions that we have asked of Him."(1 John 5:14-15).

We can be confident in our approach because of what Jesus did. He died to make us reconciled to God and co-heirs with Him. If we are asking according to God's will, He is more than pleased to give us what we ask! Praying in alignment with who and what God is, being submissive and obedient to Him, and abiding in His Word ensures that we are asking in accordance with God's will and not our own selfish desires.

Pray: Heavenly Father, we want to thank You and praise You that You have made it possible through Jesus' sacrifice for us to come with confidence before Your throne with our requests. Enable us to ask, believing, according to Your will, knowing You will hear and answer with what is best for us. In Jesus' name, amen.

Ask: Am I praying in alignment with God's will or out of my own selfish desires?

_____

_____

_____

Apply: Consider your motivations for your most recent prayers. Do you need to repent? Spend time with God in prayer and in His Word. Find a minimum of three verses that support selflessness and submission to God.

_____

_____

_____

Reflect: What happened? Tell the story of how your prayer life has changed!

_____

_____

_____

_____

_____

Intentional

Serving the Church

But in fact God has placed the parts in the body, every one of them, just as he wanted them to be. If they were all one part, where would the body be? As it is, there are many parts, but one body. If one part suffers, every part suffers with it; if one part is honored, every part rejoices with it. 1 Corinthians 12:18-20, 26

Many people in the church serve out of obligation or necessity. If you ask around, you find that the 80/20 rule is in place in the church, just like in other areas. In other words, 80% of the work (or service) is accomplished by 20% of the people. When some of God's people make excuses not to serve, the work and service required becomes a burden to those that do. In most churches, there are plenty of opportunities for service. But, they should be prayerfully considered as not everyone is suited to all positions. For example, the qualifications of deacons not only includes their character and conduct but that of their *wives* as well. (1 Timothy 3: 8-13)

God expects all believers to serve Him, and use the talents and gifts He has given them, to honor and glorify Him and promote His kingdom. To refuse is to grieve the Holy Spirit. What talents and gifts God gives you will be different from what He gives me. Just as the body is not made entirely of hands or mouths, but of different parts that work together for the benefit of the whole, our talents and gifts work together with others so that the Church (the body of Christ) is benefitted. Therefore, pray to discern God's will before accepting a position. Serve Him in the Holy Spirit. In your service to Him, the Church will be served.

Prayer: Holy Father, thank you for giving me the opportunity to serve with You where You are. Show me the area You want me to serve wit You in. Enable me through Christ to honor You with you service. In Jesus' name, amen.

Ask: Am I serving where God has called me? Do I need to step out of a position so that God can fill it with someone He has chosen?

_____
_____
_____

Apply: Answer the questions and respond according to what God speaks to your heart.

_____
_____
_____

Reflect: What happened? Tell the story of your obedience to God's directions.

_____
_____
_____
_____
_____
_____

What Interferes With Worship

Now as they went on their way, Jesus entered a village. And a woman named Martha welcomed him into her house. And she had a sister called Mary, who sat at the Lord's feet and listened to his teaching. But Martha was distracted with much serving. And she went up to him and said, "Lord, do you not care that my sister has left me to serve alone? Tell her then to help me." But the Lord answered her, "Martha, Martha, you are anxious and troubled about many things, but one thing is necessary. Mary has chosen the good portion, which will not be taken away from her." Luke 10:38-42

As we have already discussed, worship is reverence and adoration for a deity (our God). So what interferes with worship? Taking our focus off of God and putting it elsewhere. For instance, that lady with the tattoo, the teenager with the short skirt or low cut top, our lack of funds for the offering plate or our worries about our job/family/finances/friends/marriage/etc./etc./etc.

Remember when I said "Whatever you dwell on you serve"? Make sure that when you are in worship, you are IN worship. Ask God to clear your mind, clean your heart, and keep your focus on Him alone. Remind yourself of the *purpose* of your worship -- respect and love of God. Don't allow outside influences and judgmental attitudes to interfere with your worship. Repent and focus on God.

Prayer: Father, forgive me for allowing myself to be distracted by things around me and thoughts within me. Clean my heart and clear my mind so that I can focus on worshipping You as You deserve. In Jesus' name, amen.

Ask: What attitudes or distractions do I need to repent of?

_____

_____

_____

Apply: Spend quality, quiet time with Jesus repenting and listening for His direction. Be obedient to what He tells you to do.

_____

_____

_____

Reflect: What happened? Tell the story of how your worship was sweeter with Jesus.

_____

_____

_____

_____

_____

_____

Studying God's Nature

The Lord is not slow to fulfill his promise as some count slowness, but is patient toward you, not wishing that any should perish, but that all should reach repentance. 2 Peter 3:9

Studying God's nature is a great way to get to know who God is and what He is about. It is also likely to really open your eyes and bring conviction to your heart. Studying the nature of God challenges us to examine our own nature in comparison to Jesus. God's plan is to make us more like Him. The Bible says in 1 John 3:20,

> "Beloved, now we are children of God; and it has not yet been revealed what we shall be, but we know that when He is revealed, we shall be like Him, for we shall see Him as He is."

"WE shall be like Him". Study the nature (attributes of God) to better understand who God is what He is trying to do in your life, then make the choice to allow Him. He is going to accomplish His plan (Job 42:2; Ps 138:8). Choosing to work with God as He transforms your life deepens and sweetens your relationship with Him.

Prayer: Holy Father, guide me to better understand who You are and how You want to change me to be more like You. I am choosing to work alongside You as You transform my nature to be like Yours. In Jesus' name, amen.

Ask: Do I know God well enough to understand what He is trying to do in my life?

___

Apply: Study the attributes of God. Begin with the list below, find at least three verses, in context, that explain or demonstrate each attribute. Ask God how to apply this to your life:

Absolute	Holy
Loving	Immutable
Just	Omnipotent
Omniscient	Sovereign

Reflect: What happened? Tell the story of how your life is changing based on what you are learning.

___

Witness in Waiting

I waited patiently for the Lord; he turned to me and heard my cry. He lifted me out of the slimy pit, out of the mud and mire; he set my feet on a rock and gave me a firm place to stand. He put a new song in my mouth, a hymn of praise to our God. Many will see and fear the Lord and put their trust in him. Psalm 40: 1-3

Nothing testifies louder or witnesses greater than your attitude while waiting. Believe me, I have a lot of experience in waiting, and I have not always waited well. My tendency is to complain (why?), argue (when?), and help (how?) myself into a mess instead of being still (Psalm 46:10) and letting God go before me. (Deuteronomy 31:8).

Over the years I've waited many times for a million different things. Each time I would think to myself, "I will "wait better" this time." If the wait isn't too long, I usually do okay, but if it's going to be an undetermined amount of time, like forever, I start getting antsy and trying to "help". Never a good idea. [God created the world without my help or opinion so He can handle my waiting situation].

This time around, so far, I've done better. I still feel a little anxious sometimes, but then I go back to the Word and remind myself what God has said, (Psalm 23; 27:13-14; 32:8; 34:4; 37:3-5, 23; 40:1-4; 91; 118:6; 119:50, 92, 165; 139; Proverbs 3:56; Isaiah 26: 3-4, 40:31.) Then, if my mind wants to keep worrying a problem like a loose tooth, I start singing and praising God. I also have Psalm 19:14 posted in a few strategic places to remind myself to meditate on what is pleasing to God.

It all boils down to what my focus is on. If my focus is on my problems, the anxiety creeps in and I argue, complain, blame others, and behave petulantly. If my focus is on Jesus, my peace in the storm is manifested and God is glorified. The world is watching. Let your witness be of God's love, mercy, and peace instead of your grumbling, griping, and complaining.

Prayer: Lord, forgive me for complaining, arguing, and trying to usurp Your authority. You have my best interest in mind; You are making me more like You, and that takes time. During this season of waiting, help me to focus on You and not on what I think I want or need. In the end, You are all I need and You are enough. In Jesus' name, amen.

Ask: What is keeping me from focusing on God instead of my circumstances?

_____

_____

_____

Apply: What am I "waiting" for right now? How does God want to use my wait for His Glory? Create a mission statement specific to this wait to remind you to keep your focus on Jesus.

_____

_____

_____

_____

_____

_____

Reflect: What happened? Tell the story of how your "waiting" changed.

_____

_____

_____

Praying in the Spirit

In the same way, the Spirit helps us in our weakness. We do not know what we ought to pray for, but the Spirit himself intercedes for us through wordless groans. Romans 8:26

Angry.

Afraid.

Grieving.

Bitter.

We have ALL been there and some may still be there. We know we need to pray, we position ourselves to pray, but the words just won't come, and we don't know where to start. We sit with heavy, aching hearts and mute minds, but we are not alone. God promised,

> "Be strong and of good courage, do not fear nor be afraid of them; for the Lord your God, He is the One who goes with you. He will not leave you nor forsake you." (Deut 31:6).

Jesus said before He ascended "And I will pray the Father, and He will give you another Helper, that He may abide with you forever, the Spirit of truth, whom the world cannot receive, because it neither sees Him nor knows Him; but you know Him, for He dwells with you and will be in you" (John 14: 16-17).

Therefore, we can pray in the Holy Spirit and He will intercede on our behalf. When we don't have the words or we are not praying for the right things, the Holy Spirit "makes intercession for us with groanings which cannot be uttered". You are never alone, God is holding you and guiding you in the way that you should go.

Prayer: Holy Father, I don't always know what to pray. Sometimes the words won't even come. But I will thank You, praise You, and depend on Your Holy Spirit to guide me. In Jesus' name, amen.

Intentional

Ask: How do I pray when my heart is so burdened I just don't have the words?

_____
_____
_____

Apply: Begin by being thankful and grateful for all you have and all you are protected from. Praise Him through your pain. Make a list of what you are thankful for.

_____
_____
_____
_____
_____

Reflect: What happened? Tell the story of your break through.

_____
_____
_____
_____

What Worship Is Not

In the same way, on the outside you appear to people as righteous but on the inside you are full of hypocrisy and wickedness. (Matthew 23:28) He replied, "Isaiah was right when he prophesied about you hypocrites; as it is written: "'These people honor me with their lips, but their hearts are far from me. They worship me in vain; their teachings are merely human rules.' (Mark 7: 6-7)

Do you think about what you are saying and doing during worship? When you sing words from a book or off a screen, do you mean it from your heart? Are you raising your hands because you are reaching for Jesus or because everybody else is doing it?

Empty word and gestures are not worship. Worship is not a song you sing or a pose you strike. Worship is an attitude of the heart. It begins when your heart and mind align in thankfulness and gratefulness for what God has done, is doing, and will do in your life. This attitude alignment leads you to want to worship and praise God in sincerity. Prepare yourself for sincere worship.

Prayer: Almighty God, I thank You and praise You for Your work on the cross that saved me and for Your work in my life that gives me purpose. Thank You for changing me to be more like You. Prepare my heart and mind to worship You in sincerity. In Jesus' name, amen.

Ask: What do I need to reconcile before I come before the Lord in worship?

Apply: Ask forgiveness, seek reconciliation, whatever the Lord answered you to do, do it, then put on some music that lifts Him up and worship!

Reflect: What happened? Tell the story of how your worship changed and how your attitude was healed and renewed.

Learning the Promises of God

"Therefore you shall lay up these words of mine in your heart and in your soul, and bind them as a sign on your hand, and they shall be as frontlets between your eyes." Deuteronomy 11:18

My insurance company offers special "membership benefits". Other organizations have partnered with them, and I have discounts available to me, through the company. All I have to do to enjoy these benefits is to show my insurance card.

For years, I never used these benefits, because I didn't take the time to learn what I had access to. The same applied to the promises of God. I hadn't taken the time to learn all the promises of God for me. I didn't know all the wonderful benefits that my membership in the Kingdom of God offered. Learning those promises have, and still is, opening my eyes to the enormous love He has for me.

Promises of love, peace, safety, and security help me banish anxiety. Promises of deliverance, hope, and faithfulness help me to trust and not doubt. If I had not invested time in learning the promises of God, I would be missing out on the peace, joy, comfort, and security God freely offers to His sons and daughters.

What are you missing out on? Dig deep into God's Word and mine it for all the treasures in it. Find your promises from God in His love letter to you.

Prayer: Heavenly Father, open Your Word to me so that I understand Your love. Show me Your promises and teach me how to apply them to my life. Thank You for Your promises. Help me to share Your promises with others so that You are glorified. In Jesus' name, amen.

Intentional

Ask: What promises does God want to reveal in my life? What promises does He want me to share with others?

_____

_____

_____

Apply: Study the promises that God reveals to you. Go to the person(s) God wants you to share those promises with and be obedient to His prompting.

_____

_____

_____

Reflect: What happened? Tell the story of how your obedience and God's promises changed you.

_____

_____

_____

_____

_____

_____

Praying Scripture

If you abide in Me, and My words abide in you, you will ask what you desire, and it shall be done for you. By this My Father is glorified, that you bear much fruit; so you will be My disciples. John 15:7-8

There are many books on the subject of praying scripture. You can find books about why to do it, how to do it, and when to do it. And, do it you should. Praying scripture is a wonderful way to connect intimately with God while keeping you focused while praying.

Praying scripture also allows us to pray more selflessly. So often our prayers are all about *us, our* situation, and how *we* are being affected. This can quickly turn into a gripe session or pity party. Finding scripture verses that address our needs also reminds us that God is sovereign and in control, and that we are not alone. If there is a scripture verse for your situation, that means someone else has also had to deal with a similar issue. (Hint: There's ALWAYS a verse, no matter your situation.)

Praying scripture allows you to use three communication devices at one time to encounter God: praying, God's Word, and the Holy Spirit. Taking advantage of these tools will help you grow closer to who God is and how He wants to grow you in your situation.

Prayer: Lord, you tell us in your Word to ask, seek, and knock (Matthew 7:7-8), and You will answer us. Teach us to pray in the Spirit on all occasions (Ephesians 6:18), that we may be transformed by the renewing of our minds(Romans 12:2), that You would be glorified. In Jesus' name, amen.

Intentional

Ask: How can I better apply Scripture to my prayer life?

_____
_____
_____

Apply: Make a list of the top 3 situations you are currently dealing with. Find at least two scripture references that address your need for each situation and compose a prayer using the verses.

_____
_____
_____
_____

Reflect: What happened? Tell the story of how your prayer life was changed.

_____
_____
_____
_____

Serving the Lost

And Jesus said to him, "Today salvation has come to this house, because he also is a son of Abraham; 10 for the Son of Man has come to seek and to save that which was lost." Luke 19: 9-10

Serving the lost is not like serving the saved. An important thing to remember when serving the lost is to show love. The Bible says in John 13:35

> "By this everyone will know that you are my disciples, if you love one another."

Only God can save the lost. Only He can draw them to Him. Our job is to simply love. We are to love others as Christ loved us so that we can demonstrate His love to a lost and dying world.

We can share our testimony, invite people to church, sing in the choir, and serve on every committee, but if we don't have love, we are serving in vain. Serving, as it is demonstrated by Jesus, is putting others needs before our own, loving without judgment, and meeting people where they are, not where we are.

Prayer: Jesus, please open my eyes to opportunities to serve with You to reach the lost. Show me how to meet them where they are. Train my heart to love without judgment. In Jesus' name, amen.

Ask: Where can I serve the lost today?

_____
_____
_____

Apply: Be obedient to what God reveals to you. Go where He says to go, say what He says to say, and do what He says to do.

_____
_____
_____

Reflect: What happened: Tell the story of how you served the lost with God.

_____
_____
_____
_____
_____
_____

Delight Yourself in the Lord

I will meditate on Your precepts, and contemplate Your ways. I will delight myself in Your statutes; I will not forget Your word.

Psalm 119: 15-16

The book of Psalm is full of promises. Well, maybe promises is not the right word. Perhaps consequences are better. We are given instructions and then told, if we choose wisely, there will be good consequences. But, if we choose poorly, there will be bad consequences. Psalm 37: 4 states :

> "Delight yourself in the Lord, and He will give you the desires of your heart".

Sounds awesome right? Anything our heart desires will be given to us. I can almost hear a sinister "Ba ha ha ha" in the background, because it is like I've found a genie in a bottle. But, you have to read that first part again. "Delight yourself in the Lord". Delighting yourself means that you find your joy, satisfaction, and pleasure in the Lord, not in those "desires of your heart".

Remember, the Bible says that "every intent of the thoughts of his [man's] heart was only evil continually" (Genesis 6:5) and that "the heart is more deceitful than all else", (Jeremiah 17:9). If we are not finding our joy, satisfaction, and pleasure in the Lord, our heart's desires will be evil, selfish, and wasteful.

God is good, not evil. When we delight in Him, His desires become our desires and *those* are the desires He wants to fulfill. If you find that your "desires" aren't being given to you, perhaps you should re-evaluate whether or not they are in line with God's desires. If you have made an idol of those desires you are not delighting yourself in the Lord, but in other things.

Prayer: Dear Lord, are my desires Your desires? Have I made any idols out of my desires? Show me, Father. Please forgive me and create in me a clean heart. Make Your desires my desires. In Jesus' name, amen.

Ask: What are my desires? Are they pure and in line with God's desires?

_____

_____

_____

Apply: Have an honest conversation with God about your desires. Repent, accept forgiveness, and move forward. Worship with honesty.

_____

_____

_____

_____

_____

Reflect: What happened? Tell the story of what changed.

_____

_____

_____

_____

_____

Prerequisites to the Promises

If we confess our sins, He is faithful and just to forgive us our sins and to cleanse us from all unrighteousness. 1 John 1:9

The Bible offers us so many wonderful promises, but most, if not all of them, come with stipulations. Prerequisites, if you will. God says I will (fill in the blank) if you will (fill in the blank). Almost always, the promises given in this manner have the prerequisite of turning back to God and away from our sin. For example, 2 Chronicles 7:14 states:

> "If My people who are called by My name will humble themselves, and pray and seek My face, and turn from their wicked ways, then I will hear from heaven, and will forgive their sin and heal their land."

God promises here if the people called by His name will "humble themselves" (recognize their position before a holy God), "pray" (communicate with Him), "seek my (God's) face" (spend quality time in the presence of God), "turn from their wicked ways" (repent), that He will "hear", "forgive their sin", and "heal their land".

He wants to be in close relationship with us and He wants to bless us. He is also a good father that understands He can't reward or reinforce bad behavior (sin). He allows us to choose. His love for us is unconditional and infinite, it had no beginning and it has no end. His promises, however, are for those willing to submit and bend their will to God's will (humble themselves) and be obedient to all God commands. The promises are available to all, but not all will redeem them.

Prayer: Holy Father, please forgive me of my sins. Draw me into a deeper, more intimate relationship with You. Lord, I humble myself before You. Help me to turn from my sin. Thank You, Father, for Your forgiveness. Show me how to seek Your face and be obedient to Your commands. In Jesus' name, amen.

Ask: Have I been seeking God's Face (His Presence) or His hand (what He can give you or do for you)?

Apply: Find 3 promises of God and study what the prerequisites or conditions are of each. Are you applying them correctly to your life? What do you need to change?

Reflect: What happened? Tell the story of how your life and study of God's Word changed.

Witness in Working

Work with enthusiasm, as though you were working for the Lord rather than for people. 8 Remember that the Lord will reward each one of us for the good we do, whether we are slaves or free. Ephesians 6:7-8

Just like our witness in waiting speaks volumes about what we really believe, our witness in working can either point people *to* God or *away* from God. If we are not "working as unto the Lord" (Col 3:23) then we may be setting a poor example for other believers and non-believers. You may thoroughly hate the job you are in, but God can use that to show others that His Grace is sufficient. That job can become a way to glorify God in the midst of suffering. Then when others see the hope that is in you, you can point them to Christ. (1 Peter 3:15).

This is not easy. No one likes being abused, nor am I suggesting that you remain in a toxic environment if you have other choices. However, sometimes we can be in a great environment, but are put in constant contact with toxic people. Perhaps, as in the case of Esther, you are in this position for a season ("for such a time as this") so that God can reach someone. God knows that you are obedient and that He can rely on you to fulfill His will.

If your working situation is less than desirable, change your perspective. Instead of acting out (what a lot of us do), look for God's purpose in your present position. You may not have a job at this time or you may be seeking a job. Continue to TRUST and God will provide. It might be at the last second, but He will come through to meet your needs. Is there a way you can glorify Him? Is there someone God wants you to reach out to? We tend to be a self-centered people, so step outside your "self" and view your work through God's eyes. Ask Him to reveal how He wants you to glorify Him to others.

Prayer: Holy Father I don't always understand why You have put me here for this season. Help me not to focus on the negatives around me, but to look for ways that I can glorify You. Thank You for making me a part of Your plan. In Jesus' name, amen.

Ask: How can I glorify God in my job today?

_____
_____
_____

Apply: Trusting God and stepping outside your comfort zone is tough and scary sometimes. Be obedient to what God is telling you to do. Listen, pray, speak, and go.

_____
_____
_____
_____

Reflect: What happened? Tell the story of how/what changed when your perspective changed.

_____
_____
_____
_____

Hanging Out With Jesus

One of my favorite things about Intentional communication with Jesus is the feeling of peace that I have in His presence. I am loved. I am accepted. I am secure. Hanging out with Jesus fulfills all the longings of my soul. I always feel refreshed and renewed if I have authentically spent time with Him.

To make the excuse that I don't have time is a lie. The truth that combats that lie is that I didn't appoint time. Communicating with my Friend by just hanging out and spending time with Him, choosing Him over a book, television, phone, computer, or work, tells Him that He is my First Love. He is of the utmost importance. When my relationship with Him is right, my relationship with others is right. In the presence of Jehovah is where I long to be.

Prayer: Holy Father, thank you for being my Friend. I am so grateful that You want to have a real relationship with me. Help me to put aside all distractions and focus on just being in Your Presence. In Your Presence there is peace. In Jesus' name, amen.

Ask: What changes do I need to make in order to prioritize my relationship with Christ?

_____
_____
_____
_____

Apply: Make a plan to prioritize your relationship with Christ and find an accountability partner to help you carry it out.

_____
_____
_____
_____

Reflect: What happened? Tell the story of how your life has changed because of your obedience.

_____
_____
_____
_____

I hope that this devotional has changed your life as much as it has changed mine. I am praying for you to live every day of your life INTENTIONALLY from now on.

Acknowledgements

This book would not have been possible without the support of my friends, church, and family.

Special thanks to the Women of Faith. Your prayers have helped to make this possible.

Thank you to Nancy for keeping my "secret".

Thank you to my husband Scott for your unwavering faith in me always.

Made in the USA
Coppell, TX
03 July 2021